FACING THE MOUNTAIN

First Warbler Press Edition 2024

Facing the Mountain: Poems on Dying and Death, Caregiving and Hope
© 2024 Linda C. Welsh

Cover and interior illustrations from Bailius Besler's
Hortus Eystettensis first published in 1613.

All rights reserved. No part of this book may be reproduced in any form or by any means, electronic or mechanical, including photocopying, recording, or by any information storage and retrieval system, without permission from the publisher, which may be requested at permissions@warblerpress.com. New York: Warbler Press.

warblerpress.com

ISBN 978-1-962572-51-4 (hardcover)
ISBN 978-1-962572-60-6 (paperback)
ISBN 978-1-962572-61-3 (e-book)

Library of Congress Control Number: 2024933546

FACING THE MOUNTAIN

Poems on Dying and Death, Caregiving and Hope

LINDA C. WELSH

CONTENTS

I. Engagement

Facing the Mountain 1
Alien World. 4
Gates 6
Bugs 8
Willing. 11
Chain Fruit Cholla 13
Inches. 15
Drawing Too Deeply 18
Making Fire in the Damp. 20
Aperture 21
Glossary of Enchantment 23
Ruminant 25
Dappled Light 27
When the Doves Stop Singing 29

II. Devotion

Not Quite 35
Threshold 38
Heartless 40
Arroyo 43
Creosote 45
Coffee. 47
Composition. 49
Her 50
Asleep. 52
Devotion 54
Palo Verde 56
Saguaro 58

Desert Torch 60
Impermanence 61
Innocence 63
Inside-out 65
Suspense 67
Molecules 70
Spinoza 72
Pilgrim 74
Ashes to Sea 77
Yucca 80

III. Emergence

Incarnate 85
Come Closer 88
Phantom Pain 89
Lonely Body 90
Water in Spain 91
Belonging 93
Linger 95
The Last Word 96
Medicine Walk 98
Electric Mound 100
All My Breaths 102
Hold Onto Me 103
Invisible Blanket 104
Refugee 106
A Spear Thrown 109
The Size of My Soul 110
Irritant 112
24 Hours 114
Wonder 116
Jasper 118
Roar 120
Constellations 122
Original Instructions 124
Caress 127

Acknowledgments 129

1. ENGAGEMENT

FACING THE MOUNTAIN

I.

It is impossibly steep
the mountain blooming
Our compulsory journey
no way around

We navigate the
scarped stony paths and
tributaries
some deep
At least we are
traveling
together

This home, its lace
curtains climbing
the wall face
Forced air heat
rising from below
evaporating the moisture
in our skin
The impossible ground
stunts our
certainty

One footstep invites the next
force of the current
beyond our crossing
Just the pursed-lip breathing
holding hands
heads above
water

2.

Just now your eyes
meet mine
like the tinder bundle captured
by the ember and
blown into flames
This conflagration a
celebration

Your gaze
timeless and whole
wellness in the absence
of a cure

3.

Everything is
extinguishable
Camels, elephants, zebras, lions,
sloths, used to roam here
Our inheritance; change

Now the wintry filaments of
ice grace
the crystalline air
The air lithe
succinct

Death lurks in the
strained eddies
of your voice like the
bleached white roots of the
cottonwood trees
long fallen and
exposed along the
river's edge

I am here
with you
willing the closed bud of
possibility to open
into the next
adventure

ALIEN WORLD

Out the fire escape
down the black stairs I drop
into an alien world
Manzanita's red skin and
woolly leaves
The Sonoran desert; its seams and folds
stitches and designs
consciousness canvas

I see the fearful fiery orb
bedding down on the
orange-drenched landscape.
Harris's hawks pull my heart
up the sandy river

I see doomed cattle
eating beavertail cactus
despite the pain
While heat gains weight igniting
red Ocotillo flowers
and my powerlessness
This desert
a rusting jasper flame

I see my reticence
the way I cover myself
burka-clad
The way I cannot touch

the beautiful feathers
of the dead bird
Squeamish and timid
outside the old Assembly
My skillfulness
like thirst sucking
on a stone

But in my imagination I become
booming wind ushering
the weight of water over the
craggy mountain
I become as transparent as the
heat's curling flames ascending
ladders of air
I enter the radiance of Cholla
a supernova in the heart and acquire
the comprehension of
the Palo Verde tree

I imagine this path curving
through my body from vulva
to crown, the snakes'
knowing winding through my canyons
of bone

And then the night sky brightens
into violet
ever more distinct constellations
thrum a strange music
unveiled
planetarium

GATES

A decaying
backpack strewn
at the entrance
to a cave
by the border
a tennis shoe
cellophane cookie wrappers
cameras on trees
A white blimp
suspended in the air
Eyes everywhere
looking for people trying to
cross into another way of
living

I knelt down in the mud
at the edge of the tank
A place to hold water
for cows
The birds swinging from the
branch ropes
private conversations
I do not understand
I watch for snakes, a rattle
heard in the mangy grasses

The Sonoran, new and alien
an invisible road

to another way of being
among the fire ants and their
cylindrical volcanos
and the white sheet-like mats of
funnel-web spiders
a distinct roundness in the middle
for retreat

After the wind-strewn Wash
undressed into shades
of orange, black, and gray
I found in my legs
a willingness to
keep pace with the
moving sun

The frequent
rusty gates
those sentinels
holding only the invitation
to inevitable aloneness
on the other side

We walk in a winding dream
Sweat and salt and silky
flower petals and I
want to live my life
with more than
Appetite

To care
To be skillful
To be wild
and free

BUGS

1.

There are always
interesting things
in his bed

Is it a piece of pecan
or something else?
Is it a mouse dropping or
chocolate cake?
Why are these crumbs always
a shade of brown or black?
Is there a secret
poop conspiracy
here?

2.

Body odors
remind me of
the microbiology class
that killed
my chance for ignorant bliss
My teacher, "Brian O'Brian"
wore a different Grateful Dead
t-shirt to class each day
He had a
prodigious collection

"Microorganisms are ubiquitous
UBIQUITOUS!" he often said
thus my mind was
opened to the world
of everywhere present
unseen things

My battle with the bugs
and beasts
raging on ever since

These critters must stay
in their respective
neighborhoods!
No poop bacteria in the
urinary tract
No hand bacteria in the
wound

I divide up the
body parts and
associated wash cloths
White towels for his face
disposable washcloths for
down below in the
nether regions

The nether regions
where all at once
I understand these
everywhere present
unseen bugs will win
in the end

3.

How I have loved the
confident, smooth, clean
surface
transparent glass
Salads of colorful
crisp vegetables
Polished wood
Flower essences

How I have loved
the crack smack of
certainty
The clean lines of
competence
Now stuck
in the unknown
mired in mystery
feelings of
grief and loss murky
all

4.

My life's maps
dissolve like paper in
the rain
I inhale
like a newborn
with no
immunity

WILLING

Up, up, up into Old Town Sausalito
light more important with each step,
as the fireball rises over
the glimmering bay

Thoughts tread old familiar pathways
to the itchy scab,
the curious tongue feeling for
the jagged place

In the company of old Oak,
red Manzanita with her haughty skin
the willing ivy's filling
of every niche

The dense curves and textures
of this steep, green world
peppered with familiar feeling
so different from the arid openness of home

So still, like the place between breaths
alive, but close to
nothingness
The heart-beating doesn't need a reason

Tomorrow, opaque like mist flowing over
the scrubby mountainside

The now, so dormant, just the traffic resounding in the
body
Is the fragrant flowering and fruiting over?

Passing by some roadside blackberries
three plump bumpy orbs
find the mouth
savoring

CHAIN FRUIT CHOLLA

I'd seen her golden
inch-long spines
in the bends of
The Boulders
Little chunks of Cholla
on my pants
my gloves and shoes
her needles
so precise

And knew her
mischievous
shining face
would end the long night
with a greeting
each morning

Sometimes so tall
twelve feet!
I could rest in her
shimmering shade
cautiously
These flamboyant beings
long lashes radiant
keen for a deeper
acquaintance

I wonder at her dainty
deadly
spongy chains
dangling
Regal and exotic
matriarch
without warmth

I think,
This is the world that is
mine
I am hers
And I keep
walking

INCHES

I cannot breathe
increasingly so
A dry cough
begins
no energy
my body
straining forward
by inches

I lock onto his feet
and follow
the rhythm and tenor
His footfalls
lull me into
compliance
I am empty, an
abandoned shell
I list around the endless
meandering path
in and out
in and out
up and down
everything
a blur and a
surrendering

He stops. I say, "What do you see?"
It all looks

like yesterday
and the day before
dull
color of dust

I try to listen
for the voice
from the brown
Gila river
my feet
feeling every stone
like the most
fragile of flowers

Everything that happened
in this distance
was allowed to happen
Nothing was forbidden
or at least the forbidden
went unchecked
unanswered
Or did it?

Consequences
inching too slowly
so as to be
imperceptible

I walk
trying to make
fire without flint,
and I wonder if I have
ever been closer to
skin so porous an

alliance forms
with the
wild

Our energies
Our resiliency
Our breath
and absolute
trust in Her
embrace

DRAWING TOO DEEPLY

I look out
onto the horizon,
this blank expanse
bleached
white thorns
white jawbone
white sand
mica
The trail
its ashy dust
inside my mouth and covering me
without

Vulture captures
my attention,
with its circling flight
Pulling my breath,
drawing my burning, withering
feet into my
sweaty body

I look at my primordial hand
the same as any
long dead
Original person
We are the same
We are all homegrown

Where else would we be from?
Our hands know it

Bloody broad brushstrokes
red sandstone formations
The rock ledge like
a face just slapped
The heat's body
my body
intransigent sun
elongating shadows

This night's distant fading colors
cat's claw and charcoal stumps
All comfort is distant
My mind fragmented
smoldering as if it could burn on
without tinder, fuel, or spark

MAKING FIRE IN THE DAMP

I search for words
to pray
What words
when common language
for god
lacks resonance?

Desert Mother
take me in your arms
Living and dying is the same in your light

Desert Mother
grant me strength
Strength to stand upright in your presence

Desert Mother
give me hope
Hope that I may play my part well

Desert Mother
embrace my inconstant mind
Let me see and feel the heartbeat of your grace

I stand in your presence
only at your mercy

APERTURE

Scarlet tanager
fan of black feathers
short broad tail
Your crimson body
an opening where light
enters
No bigger than my palm
a summer
shimmering

I tap on the closed doors
that keep their closedness
I dig for hidden meanings
that keep their hiding
Your flight adjusts apertures
of perception
Your ruby dark-eyed pulsing
a message of freedom

This betrayed landscape
It bites
It stings
It burns
It chafes
It awes

But in your vermilion gown
you take flight

A tiny torch
thrown into the dark branches,
halting my breath
Your broad bill rounding forward
shiny eyes and body like a laser,
skipping on currents of air
in the crown
of the Mesquite tree

GLOSSARY OF ENCHANTMENT

The honeysuckle vines
framing the gate waving
with welcome

Doorways,
their insatiable appetite
an invitation without
end

Evening
shrouded
in candlelight
The smooth petal closing
of the day

Your furry skin
the smell of
your curls
Our whispers in
the dark

Incense swirling
prayers on smoke
deepened attention
connection
lingering sweetness

Music—the
Empress of all
Enchantments

The empires of
Chaparral and
Brittle Bush
Cockroach and
Sandfly defying
extinction

The jasper flame of
the maple leaf
announcing
Autumn

The sturgeons return
to our rivers these
120 million years

The pull of
Return

RUMINANT

1.

The hoofed herbivore
grazing in the meadow
extracting nutrients from
twigs—fermentation in a
specialized stomach

Rumination is only good if
you have this particular
anatomy

2.

They dammed the river
all the fish, birds, and thundering
hooves disappeared
Now 50 years later
they are dismantling it
It was a mistake
A huge construct
built on mistaken beliefs
like our illusions

All the concrete things
like weather, and
forests, the predictable
tides
And breathing
become "maybes"

and "It could be"
in the great meat
tenderizer of living,
dying, and death

Do not disappear into a
strange stoicism
Please
make all the noise
you want

                                3.
Does the Monarch celebrate
its return to
Northern Milkweed?
And what about the balls
return to the child's hand
at play?

"Maybe" could represent Hope
Like maybe there is no
death—just transformation into other
shapes, energy neither
created or destroyed

High above
A plane is circling
"I'm trying," it says
"I'm trying again."

DAPPLED LIGHT

I always thought maximum light
was the key to flourishing
in the garden
But too much sun can sear tender
plants, burn leaves
desiccate trunks and branches
kill little seedlings

Too much light can kill

Now, in these shadows
I feel relief from
brightness

Now, in the freckled
light I can
take rest
Trusting

At night, traffic light
flares in the dark
Inside insight
flares, all of me
dilated

Don't be
ashamed of trying
your best and finding
it wanting
Life grows well in
dappled light

WHEN THE DOVES STOP SINGING

Every night
I crawl into
our pale
green tent
to the cooing sounds
of doves
Those long-distance flyers
with their long
necks.

I put on every
bit of clothing
I possess,
a cocoon
And wonder if the
rabbits shiver
in the clay fields?

Then comes
the long
deep silky silence
When the doves
stop singing
and the light
fades away.

Then comes
the rhythmic
sound of
your purring
and the
solitude of
sleeping last.

Then comes
the imagined
scorpion creeping over
cobbled covers.
I claim your fatal
venom as my own
medicine.

I feel thirst
which is to say
there is no purely
conceptual answer
to the problems we face.
Answers lie in real things;
the grasses,
their adaptations,
the cacti,
their versions of life in
the neighborhood.

And I believe
I have found
not my place in the world,
but the direction for
my thinking.
I feel my clenched fists

open in the
preeminence
of the
living world.

Do you feel it?
The song of your body,
the rhythm of
your becoming.

Do you see the patterns of nature?
The essence
of courage,
our essence.

II. DEVOTION

NOT QUITE

Inhaler on the night
stand
too tall canister for
arthritic hands to press
no dilating mist
for her to breathe

The tea, once hot
now cool
cup too full
for her to pick up

The bedside commode
two steps away
impossibly far and
the oxygen cord
too short for that
journey

The weight of the warm
blanket on her legs
toes pressed down
and cold

The help that comes
not quite
in time

Savory soups
simmering
no appetite

The days as long as
a giant's legs
traversing over the
mountain tops
never
arriving

The bored clicks
and grunts of the oxygen
concentrator
The fear its little engine will
fail

The way the peachy
stalks sway outside
barren ground
in between
tufts of grass
A brittle landscape

Death, your presence
brings gifts of contrast;
spruce and honey
striving and surrender
pain and relief
desperation and peace
bitter and sweet

Death, your presence
brings questions and
unknowing—
Was my life
well lived?

THRESHOLD

In birth there is pain,
relief and joy
when it goes well
always blood

In death will there be pain,
relief and joy?
Will there be a
sense of completion?
Will there be blood?

Uncle vomiting
thick mucus and bile
Poor Auntie watching
Please don't let him go out
hard

Will his death be like a little stone
skipping on the lake dissipating
sweetly without a fuss?
Or will his death
leave us all covered in
ash and dust?

This liminal space between
The past and future
This liminal space
I want to end

this threshold so empty and
so full

We squint through subtle changes
trying to see
Is it the beginning of the end?
Is it the end?
Is it the end of the beginning?
It's exhausting

The crystal light
over the sink
shines in the key
of D singing of
hope and wonder

The end becomes a
beginning
The dark gives way to
light like morning
The going is the
coming in this circle
The exit is the
entrance

HEARTLESS

I want this to be over
Do you think me
heartless?

In birthing the most painful part is
"transition"
labor to
open so
the baby can be pushed
through

At the end of life
the most painful parts of the
journey can last...
for years

It is not heartless
to wish for freedom
for the
suffering to be
over

It is not shameful
to wish for an exit
for clean hands
good smells and
time for oneself;
to wish to break the tether

that keeps us circling
around the field
devoid of grass

We remain a potential spark
quiescent like the
rising moon
like the sprout longing to awaken
ending
this dormant dailiness

And so it goes
the days adding up to
weeks and months
and still the tenuous
line to life
holds

What a powerful and persistent thing;
the beating heart
For years the electric currents flow
and boom—
it beats.

You could stand on your head
or throw yourself out of a plane
and still it beats
You could dive to the bottom
of the sea or walk into a burning building
and still it beats
You could be angry, sad, or laughing uproariously
and still it beats
This little drum does not ask for permission
and it is not interested in

convenience or
mercy

Some days can
feel like sailing
in a vast sea with
no wind

ARROYO

> Arroyos
> desert avenues
> tired veins, some
> varicose
> Remnants of
> a past happening
> each one's ground, soft
> and indifferent
>
> The driest hope,
> relief from the flat expanse;
> the steep-sided flash of a
> carved cliff,
> met me in the chapped air.
> The huge tumbling boulders
> tell of their sudden history,
> without words
>
> Salty breezes
> like a sigh
> Salt stains from sweat
> on my clothes
> I am down on my knees
> in the sparkling sand to rest
> when the copper fields surrender
> to the voices of coyote

Once, in the spring
utterly drenched in warm rain
my accordion heart
expanded
with the gift

Now, collapsed
in company with
the coyote's nimble tongues
singing their perennial
songs

CREOSOTE

Your sprigs of shiny
green leaves
tiny yellow flowers
Larrea tridentate,
always swaying
flirtatiously
in the breeze

Shade, seed food,
pollinator
I reached my hand
to touch your leafy cloak,
smell your smoky
tar-scent

I wanted to see,
to hold whatever it is
that makes you so
buttery and glossy in this
uncensored landscape,
the desert
where you want to
go on living

Passing by your
golden eruptions
leaf hands beckoning

from
branch sills

I accept your
invitation
for
a sip of
splendor

COFFEE

Flint for fire
black bean of possibility
Yawning in the dawn
Heat that forces out
the haze

Aroma swirls like
incense smoke
smoldering motivation
The brief heaven
of savoring

Slowly
I awaken to
the quiet fury of
change polishing the
edges of
us

Slowly
I awaken to
the citrus pucker of
bird language outside
chirp, cackle, and caw

I awaken to the
enchanting
song

of wind combing the
Bristlecone Pine

I awaken to the need for
surrender
Surrender to the
timing of events,
to the way of this landscape we
are moving through,
its spits and cries
flinching and
body empty of
possibility

You say, "hold my hand
I want to be part of you"
and we hold
Oh we hold and wait
at the altar
of time

You say, "I feel ready"
and we feel
Oh we feel wholehearted in this
unknowing

You say, "Thank you"
and we open like
window glass that lets in
the sun

COMPOSITION

I play a drum with deep tones vibrating
As I play you say
It is you

You play a piano like a harp
As you strum
I say it is I

You orchestrate the piece
Its dynamics and tempo
I offer my instrument

I play the drum with my hands
the metal edge keeps clanging in
My fingers bruise

You play the piano like a harp
strings keep fraying and snapping
in your hands

We rewrite
We stay
We play on

HER

The long hairs on
her arms, like sparse
Joshua Tree on
the arid plain,
and the lone fine hair
growing from the center of
her forehead—
a playful bindi.

Her jagged nails, the clippings
falling on the rust and brown towel,
the colors of a forest floor
Her skin, hair, and nails
filled with joy
and desire without end!

The purple plum bruises
covering her body
like honeysuckle vines in bloom
spiraling
a trellis

Her cultured
manner
and feral spirit in
perfect communion
The seed of her

a universe encased
in skin.

Her skin, the smell of
musk and melon
Her vibe,
acoustic
guitar

Her lovers and
their gifts—paintings,
statues of the Buddha,
platters and crystal vases,
tiffany lamps, necklaces,
earrings, and perfumes,
vestiges of color
cheering her on

So much unsaid
that will never be
said
So much said
that will never
be unsaid,
just the
coda
bringing her passage
to a close

Now, her pale face
and persistently red
lips
oxygen ornament
pianissimo

ASLEEP

Is death like
falling after losing hold
of the cliff edge,
losing foot placement
on the rock ledge,
eyes filled with
sand?

Is dying a
clinging, sweating
desperation with stretched out
dread before the
collapse of clutching?

Or is death as kind as
falling asleep?
Not that terrifying
version of
stranded doom
without choice.

Is death a back float in
buoyant water
effortless
where breathlessness is not a
choking struggle
but a different kind of
inhalation and exhalation;

an easeful one without
coughing, without
air hunger's
clawing?

Is death like
the heavy gray clouds
that move through
a change becoming
rain?

Is death an opening
and entering?
An entering and joining?
A joining and awakening?
A soft landing someplace
new?

DEVOTION

Sometimes
a surprising bitterness swells in me
salivating as from
the thought of a
lemon

So much suffering in
our stories
It doesn't matter if they are
true or not

You, you, you
begin all the blaming chapters
You did, you did not do
punishing, criticizing, accusing
You, you, you

My reverie interrupted
by your needs now
Your need and
my aversion both
irritating
What a messy palette of
feeling

Beloved,
I also remember the
rumble of your

voice
your smile the day
we met
You, you, you
The texture of your
skin against mine
The well-trodden path of
our days
together

Our story,
its swells and depressions
seem to return to a sea
of pages where we might
rewrite the telling of it with
greater appreciation

Life unfolds just
beyond the reach of
my powers
Beloved, I concede

All the exquisite
pieces fill the time capsule
hidden until the end of walls

I thank you
I love you
I forgive you
Please forgive me

This time made
sacred
by devotion

PALO VERDE

Your flowers come
when water is enough
your whole jade body
capable of
transforming light

Flowering waves
crash puffy yellow
prancing
over your green-like-no-other
chlorophyll shores
a conflagration for bees

Plump seeds waiting for
the foragers
the seeds
currency in this
full on
depression

Your mothering
assuages the
punishing toll of
heat and drought
dark wreckage
becomes possibility
in your shade

How I would love to
photosynthesize!
How I would love to
speak your incantations!
How I would love to
master your instruments!

I found a wish
in my chest at dawn
bubbled its way
to the fore of my mind and
into the day;
to join the Palo Verde
choreography
outside the icy tent

SAGUARO

Consider the kingdom of Saguaro
acrobats with their
comedic routines
Columns of mellow green tissue
dressed in protective spines
White flowers in late spring
Red fruit in summer

It can take you 150 years to say
what's on your mind
200 years to perform
your burlesque show
You will be here when we
are long dead

Infallible sense of water
capture
You grow sweetly
rich and wild
among the
waterless rivers

I look inside the
round nest entrance
Shadows inside like
a pecan pie
You are
host to Gilded Flickers

Woodpeckers
Owls
Finches
Sparrows

I touch the kaleidoscope
tips of your arms
cottony white symmetry
with thorns
I look, mesmerized
into this perfection
pure white
sacred geometry
unfurling

I sit at your feet
The barely perceptible sway
of your column
The lead blanket
of your weight
calm and unhurried
rocking me
to sleep

DESERT TORCH

Spiky asymmetry
like a pile
of sheet music
Each branch its own
tune

Sprays of brilliant red flowers
Neighborhood graffiti
written on
the walls of
the sky

Atop your lanky stems
flares for hummingbirds
and bees

Your branches make shade
structures
Your spindles, like
frozen water fountains of
green and gray

Tell me how you
live in the crisp
callous world
making sugar
without leaves?

IMPERMANENCE

The flower arrangement wilts
white petals turn inward
the stamen of the Lily
spread their rust dust
on my knitted sweater

Yellow rose petals rimmed in maroon
fall on the cream countertop
their green leaves strain toward
amber

I take some earth and
coffee grounds and fill
a crystal dish
chop the petals with a fast knife
colors blend in yellows,
reds, and a dash of green;
Birth, growth, and
flowering

This mandala, a launch pad
for our prayers that rise
on smoke
I hold a bronze singing bowl
inlaid with a brass Buddha
The hand-carved mallet
covered in smooth leather

We bow our heads
raise our hands
let the mallet strike
the purest sound
reverberates
then fades

INNOCENCE

There are places in the
world that are
in-between where nothing is
either good nor bad
light nor dark, fair nor foul
right nor wrong

There are no rules
there are no norms
there are no boundaries
there are no individuals
only choices

Do I give another pain pill now?
Do I push fluids?
Do I feed less, feed more
stimulate less, stimulate more
turn him less, turn him more
touch him less, touch him more?

Just the tides
the moon rise
carving winds
the icicle rain
the weathering
the eroding
the breathing
the enduring

We are innocent
innocent as
the clocks' face

INSIDE-OUT

I wait in
this stillness
How much energy
it takes
to do
nothing

On the inside
uncomfortable with
uncertainty and
powerlessness
as if I too am limited by
the enclosure of his bed
rails up
or my own
mortality

Am I doing the work of becoming
or am I married to this
entropy?
I make room for visitors among
the syringes, catheters, and sweet foods
I make room for pleasantries among
the red plaid blanket, paisley pillows,
pink Easter bunny, and
absolute stasis

I make tunnels in the silence with Debussy
I open the simple windows edge
I open the curtains their lids blinking

In drops the ornament of lemon sun
I call to this morning as spring!

I open the door and feel the swagger of leaves!
I call to the waves and flap of wings;
the cooing doves in the Oak tree,
the immense seductiveness of
sailboats, and traffic clatter
Bay tree and eucalyptus scent
just outside

SUSPENSE

Does dying poorly
give me a demerit on my
life's report card?
Does it work that way?

What was the meadowlark's
feeling before I found her
lying in the field?

Is there a special timing to
leaving?

Is there something I must
do or say?
Some lesson I am meant to
grasp?

I have no energy
Just my shallow breaths connected
to legs that
are weak
and a rib cage that no longer swells
with air

I like the phrase, "there is no place to
go and nothing to do"
But a part of me feels
exceedingly restless like

a letter A in search of B or the
number 1 in search of 2 and 3

I am ready to launch
but don't know how?
My heart keeps
beating
There is no on/off switch
in my body
just a very slow march to
shut down

I'd like to expedite the
progression of events
The suspense is
killing me!
The changes to
my body proceed
onward
I do not recognize my
face
Such an illusion the
body's permanence
Do these changes count
as dying?

I strain for clarity but
lapse so easily into
absurdity

This rowing labor
working to move toward
the other shore

Inside I am as pure as
the tone resounding from
the brass singing bowl
untouched
by this
transformation

MOLECULES

I live
on the surface
of an orb spinning in
a vast universe

Molecules charged
with attraction
cross the synapse
making the long journey across
the expanse to port
at a dock that fits them
perfectly—Bang! The impulse
launches

The chair that holds me
feels solid but is
mostly empty space
The skeeter walks
on water as if
it were
land

These small miracles
These mysteries
This world, its
magnificence
invites the

loosening of a singular
identity

Loving with the lovers
Playing with the
children at play
Grieving with the weary
Crossing with those who
cross over
Savoring what it feels like
to be alive

The systems of the body divided
into organs, organs
into cells, cells
into atoms, atoms like the
stars above me

In the final interview
of me and my parts
some will not show up
at all

SPINOZA

*"All happiness or unhappiness
solely depends upon the quality
of the object to which we are attached by love."*
—*Spinoza*

The hooked knife
of memory
sharp and unrepentant
threatens my sleep
Images flash
How I love you
repeating

Memory foam pillow
pink salt lamp
silky blanket
chain on the ceiling fan clicks
its tune
The inextinguishable yellow
walls

Outside the leafy heads of trees
nod their airy indifference
Inside a fountain of scents
images and remembrance
flood the room
The redwood floor

petrified pillars
legs and arms and
necks of wood

I wait for the ripening
of your illness
The final fruits
I will pick
and eat
and be nourished
by

Anything having
to do with
You
I will
savor

PILGRIM

I wake early
descend the stairs to look
for breath
for discomfort
his heart like
a little bird
beats
one hundred and thirty times a minute

The years dressed in
tautness and weight
His skin pale, smooth, and cool
His toothless mouth
shut tight

I wash his face and hands
I kiss his head
no response

I worry
about his back
the tender skin there
doing all the
work of containing

I worry about his bowels
that have not moved
for days

I worry about the body
stiffening while living
I worry there is pain I cannot
discern
I worry he will not pass while
I am here
and the long epilogue will
continue even after there
are no pages left
The exhausted writing going on
like contrails in an azure sky

And then fears become
more existential
argument
more insistent

Dying is incontrovertible

He seems to float
Not here or there
I look for every twitch or
blue sound
Then wonder if my
scrutiny is disturbing?

I worry he has no place
to land
As if flying over a sea
that he is circling with no fuel

No prayer for mercy seems to
land anywhere either
as if God is indifferent and time is

meaningless in this space

These thoughts
the wringing of hands

I look to him for instruction
but he is silent
Just the flow of breath
his mouth a doorway

I try on
the stiffness
the inability to move
the utter weight of absent energy

I smooth his neck though
in health he did not like
to be touched

ASHES TO SEA

Salty sailor
graying beard
Calabash pipe
smoke spiraling
His den an homage to
years at sea
Ships he sailed pictured
on the wall from
1944

A library of Classics
carefully curated
Treasured bookends from
various ports
carved gourds, claws,
a silver dagger
Hundreds of clippings of articles
carefully filed
We were more articulate before
communication in bits and bytes

He walked to the
Sausalito ferry each day
whistling
he told me once

Patrick, happily walking along
the bay, sometimes stumbling

Guinness-full
his internal life booming like
wind in the sails of a
Clipper Ship

The immensity of his life
on the inside
Little movement from without
Few words, few expressions, few efforts
at engagement or connection

The diminishment of his body seemed
to have little effect on his Self
All the trips to the hospital
increasing dependencies
indignities
The slow closing of doors
leading away from his
railed bed

Life came to a close like a
Seagull silently circling the cliffs
Its wingspan extended in the glide
His shallow breaths and mouth
an oval opening
pouring itself back
into the sea

The bell on the ship
rang solemnly as
his ashes met the waves with
marigold, eucalyptus, and salvia petals
off the coast of Kirby Cove

Sinking into the sea
his weight remembered
The falls, the turning, the changing
of clothes and baths
All-through-the-night padded underwear
The weight of his silences
The weight of his introvertedness
The light of his dimples and shiny eyes
His chuckle at Charlie Chaplin movies
His savoring of salmon and chocolate,
books, travel, and the night sky
All sinking down and into
Everything

YUCCA

                      1.

The black cow is panting
agonal breaths
in the heat
She is lying in a rut
feet pointing up
an embankment
She breathes through her
flared nostrils
spraying mucus
I try to give her water
she can hold

The land
rutted and rank
Blanketed in
piles of dung
eroded formations
pointing up
breathe fast
in the heat then
turn cold

                      2.

I would love to live
in a world of humans

frolicking in conspiracy
with green leaves
and sheep
Straw bales and lodge poles
and earth
Little Wikiups
of sculpted clay
each with its own
warm light
embedded in a garden

I would love to flourish
in the orchestra of
rhythmic steps
Trekking poles and footfalls
the muscle of patience
crunching gravel
the clicking and clucking
on the rocks
soft music
In the company of the
Beloved

                              3.
Is passionate expression
not stuck in human concrete
possible?
Can appetites and desires
be a force for more life
found ferocity?
What will I do?
What will I not do?

4.

Timidity and docility
the shallowness of life
lived in exile
from the sentient world

5.

Have you ever seen
anything more cuttingly exquisite
A Yucca bloom
steaming upward on its
magic carpet
It's perfect wholeness
sharp and tender
petals?

Moths pollinate
birthing Yucca flowers
this lovemaking
And the moths themselves
could not
exist were it not for the
Yucca flowers

Theirs is an
extremely specific
and prolific
Mutualism

III. EMERGENCE

INCARNATE

1.

I step into the cooked landscape
Where the long wait
has ended

Unmoored
at sea in the
desert

2.

I pour the story of myself
into the sandstone hollows
existence in this expanse
a mirage

Vulnerable stuck and struck
by thorns
How insignificant
my machinations

Turned inside-out my lung tissue
reflected in the desiccated
beavertail cactus

Red Tail Hawk
surveying the scene
Hers is the whole
sky

3.
Does life regret
our existence?

4.
Thirst and this prickly world
I let go of the life
I have known
Memories of self-gratification
like bird nests
in the Cholla
safe
well placed
intentional

Smells of dying and death
newborn calves
left to perish
The frank facts of their
worthlessness
masturbating
in the open

We could have
saved them

5.
The windblown
arms of trees
wind incarnate
Manzanita this evening
flames incarnate
Decomposing plants
future earth

6.

The waste of my love
spilling over
the only moisture
here

COME CLOSER

Night and sea ripple and flow like old window glass
All at once, the gull from docks away
takes flight

The thrum of trucks and television
the splashing of water breaking
A cocoon of caring for other than my own, made my own

The oak trees so manicured, their branches tamed
perfection
Lights in houses glow blue where families have what they
need
Apparently

This is my story, a way to document my madness
Knowing in the course of these meanderings I will not
arrive
I walk as if the road could guide me

All at once, a lonely feeling flutters
A clench of fear. But the air is sweet with Bay scent.
The ivy thrives
on the steepest of cliffs

The heavy gleam of my eyes falls
I can be nothing but flesh in the body of the Earth
And I think I am all right again

PHANTOM PAIN

In the open space of possibility
I walk along the bay
my hungry beggar eyes find every pair
of clasped hands every
white-haired couple entwined
in their long years every
bicycle built for two

How I remember the feeling of having four limbs
the joy and weight of this balance

Now, in the slow, cool evenings I feel the
phantom pain of the sick severed limb

It aches from its place on the other side of the veil
It calls to me saying, "My absence will always pulse
in you singing."

LONELY BODY

Lonely body
vine design etched
along driftwood bones
where kisses once took root

Through the lens
images bubble up from the sandy shore
bursting their radiant message
Love was a sailor in this harbor

Drenched in remembrance
Searching for the lighthouse
I watch excluded and enamored
the seafaring of one I loved

Accepting the fine point
that love set sail
I was entered and the sweet
syrup flowed out to the incandescent sea

And that waves return
Tides come in
The sand is lit up
by the persistent moon

I loosen myself like sea foam
My lonely body floods again

WATER IN SPAIN

Wedged between Germany on the bunk above
and Canada on the bunk below
Our metal raft drifting on the creaky floorboards
Hairs caught in mattress springs
A dim-lit room in contrast to a brilliant day's end

Swishy sounding sleeping bag tumbled in a ball
not just its weight matters
but years of baggage like the pollen sacks of bees
clinging to the body of my story what
will I make of it in the alchemy of the road?

I walk and walk and walk across a country with
my well-read thirst
Listening to the story line in my mind
Characters make their entrances and exits with a backdrop
of absolute
newness, mountain splendor, a path whistling forward
endlessly

At the entrance to every little village
a fountain
Fresh flowing water, cool—all I can drink
My parched bewilderment and the Play with the dried-up
ending
watered by these flowing fountains

Walking rhythm snags my wonder
All around colors layering from pine to butter
The rain cloud bursts its feelings
I raise my cup expectantly
while the fields flood untamed

BELONGING

I walked naked and loose through
the cottage door
Pine boughs courting the gusty air
in the crescent moonlight

A Phantom takes flight!
We have surprised each other;
a Great Gray Owl swoops down
between the dark trunks of the fir trees
weightless, fierce, indifferent
the soundless span of his wings
enveloping the air
my breasts quivering
He vanishes
into the open field
gray merging into black

I remember you swooping down and in
between dark vegetation, my precise path
We have surprised each other;
My loamy body, porous against the velvet blanket, you
weightless, fierce, indifferent
the span of your arms
enveloping me
Your eyes a cymbal splash
vanishing into the open field
gray merging into black

Astonishment taste in my mouth
is all that's left of your kiss
and the Owl's return

LINGER

A love garden between us
We linger in the summer heat
Evening turns cold with our uncertainty
It could end, our paradise is capable of devastation
All, all can be lost

Through juniper scented air
the smoke columns indifferently rising
and beyond
a smoldering field
of regret

The skin keeps a little of life with you
The mouth not even that much
The heart is different
It persists not
whole and not dead

Impermanence the strand gleaming
I open for her
showing her the fabric of my own heart
fabric like her presence
swaddling me

THE LAST WORD

The contrite fir forest
an icy, achy world
Her breath freezes just as it
passes her lips
and falls, crystalline to the heaving ground

Her footfalls crunch
The snow like shards of glass
When the way to fulfillment
cannot be conceived

Bitter stillness strangely inviting
A door ajar
She wraps herself in boldness
arranges herself on the teetering chair
listening to the air being still

She is a defiant verse
Her body the way to speak
to an oppressive regime that
broke its own rules

Will dissent take this singular shape,
a form dangling,
a wind chime in an unsympathetic landscape
singing but breathless?

The rope cuts where
she has been weak
Oh the allure of having the last word
Of becoming the frayed cloth glistening
in the feathery air

MEDICINE WALK

    Listen, eyes closed

    Let pleasure open you
    creative energies flow
    through your own channels

    Let satiety, bliss bring you
    into the cello and bow tango
    of the divine
    Let the pinched, hypoxic feeling pass
    a cloud

    Tune in, pen in the air

    Your electric circuits a home
    Curiosity the mouth entrance
    Sit at the table of your safe pulse waiting
    Feel solar plexus ignition

    Kindle your flames
    Delight is the tinder, happiness the spark
    Do not grow cold! All the makings
    of fire surround you

    Keep going, your tongue clucking

    Do not fear the haggard and hunched
    presence of disappointment

Paucity of opportunity
a mirage

The weight of suffering lives
in your stories
The oval craving sounds
Feel the answer
inside

ELECTRIC MOUND

I am like the person who learns to read
by circling letters on the page
Letters whose sound I know
like "T" for two

Before, I thought my life could be lived in him like
the inner radiance of the persimmon encased in skin
Now I see my ripeness is married to decay, both
add to life and come to know death

I pretend to be whole and satiate while
feeling as transparent and permeable as a cell
and inconstant as seaweed moving back and forth
over the contradictions

My steady companions; the heart bleating, the breath
a little rhythm section
all its own
The whoosh of blood throughout

My ecology
my electric mound and shrugging folds
my pools of being
even the gremlin mind striking continuously at the past

And down below the way the fleshy roots seek
the way the chair and mat and pillow preside

the weight of the cat's head in my palm
the way I sail without seeing you

ALL MY BREATHS

When I die will they add
up all my breaths to see if they amount
to a life well lived?

Will they see an absence of width
or an absence of depth?
Will they see how I struggled toward a deeper discharge
toward a more complete letting go,
toward being able to sleep comfortably on the uncovered ground,
or touch the urine-drenched sheet with my bare hands?

Will they notice my determination
like a clap of scent pulling me onward?
I have never slayed the malady
the feeling that I was made of mirrors
reflecting everything but rarely seen

When they untie the twine
of my dead fingers from the list of achievements
will they find the story of that longing part—
my heart?

HOLD ONTO ME

The garden bursting into flame and the lovemaking
floret nipples and silky areola petals
The air heavy with bees

The little sprouts
thrusting themselves toward the
light again. Their flares easing out
from the downy darkness moist
Each seedling glistening

This new life, the color
of the leaf, her long veins, her arousal
I bow to this brightness
Loving has no wrong season

I am made of this; soil, water, light
The way your smells enter me
the weight of bones and blood
a blanket fraught with meaning
and purpose

Hold onto me as the force rises
The sweat of metamorphosis on my cheek
This brief moment when the mind
is here and I am part
of it; the body of the world
my body

INVISIBLE BLANKET

Creaking black swivel chair, tired brown chest
Aching knee
Sunlight passing through the lens that
changes shape to focus
tries to see

Bodies of long dead organisms unceremoniously exhumed
Now black coal, black oil, and gas combust

We burn the old bodies, cheap energy
Machines of industry grind out cement
In kilns building blocks bake
We build civilization
We build civilization, powerfully

The rabid release of carbon dioxide rises skyward
And downward, ever onward

An invisible blanket
makes us warmer, ever warmer
Scientists who vigil at life's edge
casting back in time
forward toward projections

Even they are unmoored
Respect carbon dioxide

Invisible like radio waves carbon dioxide dissolves in
seawater
changing the careful chemistry of the seas
the vast aquarium we too are swimming in
Wake up! The oceans are becoming
more acidic

Will the habit of ourselves steal
the wealth from our purse?

With carbon dioxide plants make the sweet
sugars on which our lives depend
We breathe it, our relations breathe it in
We are adding carbon dioxide to the atmosphere
pouring it into an already full cup

The system I was born into and perpetuate
Apprehension wild as an untethered colt, yet enclosed

It's the wild rose with her five pink petals that tug this tale
It's her scent that brings me to where
fires are raging
Air is brown and my mouth too tastes
of ash

REFUGEE

I.

I sang in the sun
naked squeals of delight
sustenance and ponies

Then I sang and paraded for
ideas of salvation
loving kindness and peace

I studied about tyranny
and your struggle
Distant martyrs

I studied about
my invisible backpack
privilege

Now I sing in my garden
about what threatens you
Your suffering

I sing in a tentative voice
about what I have never
lived

I sing about being haunted
by your unattended children

and my powerlessness
I sing our simple duet
trying to hear
your voice

My mind small and my tune
shrunken to its size
I sing my fleeting
gladness in the callous
landscape of this world

2.

After you left us for good
The mosaic ground baked and cracked
The soil pulled up her skirts and spirited away
The desert laid claim to what was once fertile
saying, "mine."

With my six legs; survive, eat, family, hunger,
guns, collapse, I crawled into the dusty camp
and became, for awhile a wooden statue for some to
feel shade

And then I made of myself a wooden spoon
serving out rice water to swollen bellies
and glazed-over eyes

3.

In my dreams, I am a bird. I fly with hundreds
toward vast fields of wetlands, our migration
rewarded with food, drenched delight
My wings trail in the waters leaving ripples
that tease turtles and bugs

When I wake to these stiff sullen bones
I hear
keep going

A SPEAR THROWN

Time is blooming
What does this feeling
Know?
Go beyond

Could I sing, scream, belt out more?
Could I say what all the parts want to hear
and release all the birds captive
in my heart?

Can I transform, metamorphose?
Am I made to dissolve within a silken
tomb and turn into
something else?

Not quite ready to
concede
I wade into
the lavender sea

I dive through the center
of this square moment
my face like
a spear thrown

THE SIZE OF MY SOUL

Next time I will bury hope in a pine box ceremoniously

notice the face, what makes the eyes glisten
the lines around the mouth
what furrows the brow
how the voice rises
whether this animal is
a fish to my camel

Next time I will know the truth before I ask you

listen to the rumpled sheets
whether the conversation quells my breath or enlivens it
whether the house has hooks that can hold the size of my soul
whether this animal is
an eagle to my mouse

Next time I will see if there are love gifts or affirming words

I will believe what you say about yourself
Listen to the emerging patterns and emanating aromas
Look for the generous impulse, consciousness awakened
whether this animal is
a frog to my antelope

Next time I will listen to my marrow being still

See the shape of facts and not look away smiling
not wait too long, my lips puckered in the air
Do the thirsty work of love
but not in the hospital of the naïve
whether this animal is
a turtle to my cheetah

Next time I will be the empress of my own world

I will bathe your feet
Bear witness to your unfolding
Celebrate your wild and singular life
relishing

IRRITANT

My eyes burn upon rising
My eyes burn when the image of the
man lying in the middle of the sidewalk
strange tight blue plastic gloves on his
Super-hero-stranded hands
presses on my iris.

My eyes burn when I take a shower
Are any of these things in our water:
Arsenic pdf, Bacteria, Benzene pdf, Boron pdf,
Dibromo-3-chloropropane (DBCP) pdf,
Hexavalent Chromium (Cr 6) pdf, Lead pdf,
Mercury pdf, Methyl tert-Butyl Ether (MTBE) pdf,
Nitrate pdf, N-nitrosodimethylamine (NDMA) pdf,
Perchlorate pdf, Perfluorooctanoic Acid (PFOA) pdf,
Radionuclides pdf, Salinity pdf,
Tetrachloroethylene (PCE) pdf,
Trichloroethylene (TCE) pdf,
1,2,3-Trichloropropane (TCP) pdf,
1,4 Dioxane?

It's not normal to live in fear of the
water from the tap

Not at peace. Starving for action that ripples beyond my
fleeting life

Not at peace. Seeing what lives outside of my own bias
Not at peace. Pushing beyond the paralysis of being momentary

My eyes burn

24 HOURS

Yesterday
When I go to you at night
along the road of regret, I say
I did not fold my body and pass
it through the narrow opening

Then I laugh
my head thrown back

Today
Silver hair on my head
eyes dry and heavy with concern
eyebrows sparse like the broken lintels
of a house
settling down

Inside life force animating
retrospective data informing
And the fox's focus
tail fluffy as a cloud

Tonight
Tonight these lovers will visit;
the wind, the smoldering fire
the book unopened

Tomorrow
The kiss and slap, the striving and collapse, the sore feet and cravings, the abandonment and grieving, the laces and zippers, the soaps and garden, the effort and surprise, the loneliness and berry picking, the ambition and dancing, the clicks and snorts, the hairbrush and sweating, the vegetables and overgiving, the desires and muscle, the distance and intimacy, the promises and demands, the resignation and determination...

WONDER

There's a woman now
walking a path along the edge of land
through the tangled Podocarp forests
across some impossible water body between
gritty, rugged shores. Miles of it. The land is
constantly prickly and her body too is pricked
by it.

Her mind is filled with voices all swirling together
in the cacophony of the waves, rampant roots,
Opossum screech
pondering the ultimate truism:
"It depends."

I love to see her working her way to this excruciating
relentless project from the more uncomfortable and
inexorable
work assignment where the dream was born
See her stumbling to the end of the trail,
inflamed body
smiling.

Of course this is how
I have experienced love—something of wonder
and unreasonable challenge
Harder to attempt once you've known the numbing
tiredness, the unrelentingly rugged terrain,

The white flag raised unable to soothe the place your ferocities meet
And you choose to go anyway.

JASPER

He sets up shop outside of Walgreens
Brown skin and graying hair
speaking his sweet music like a clock, "Hi
cinnamon and sugar. It's fine
to be kind, bada bing!"
His partially missing two front teeth covered in silver
His smile a tinsel curiosity

Sometimes he falls asleep there
on his camp chair, sometimes
he dries his socks and his shoes, at home
on the north side of the bus stop Polk St.
What does Jasper know about eyes?
The way they dart away or blandly disappear him
The disdainful eye, the contemptuous eye, the eye
repulsed

What does Jasper know about faces?
The way they pinch up, skin taught with apprehension
Or the way some meet his eyes and nod unafraid
or share a banana and some coins

His life on the sidewalk, transparent and exposed
His reserve stretched over too much bone
One reason for all striving
Everything we are running from

What does Jasper know about the city; its creaks and

groans
its grinding gears?
The exhaust and horns honking, the pace, the urgency
the dog and human shit gauntlet, the gaudy buildings race
for the sky

Is it music? Could we break out
in a dance in this drowned balance
Jasper and me and the pigeons roosting
on his legs?

Is he a cog in the wheel of industry, am I?
Are we an organ of the city's activity, where
nothing is trying very hard to be equitable or kind?

Is he lubrication or motivation? Am I?
Is there a mistake in the cloud gap where
the sun floods through?

It happens effortlessly and predictably
His silver smile
"Bada bing!"

ROAR

    I turn to the howling coyotes
    I raise my head and make my soul sound
    My world hears
    I make my soul sound

    I turn to the lightening
    Insight flash
    Heat for alchemy
    Flame out of which to rise cleansed

    I turn to the greatness of day and night
    I wait in a helpless way
    Awkwardly
    not awake and not asleep

    I turn to the miracle of
    cell division
    I am in the musky soil
    pushing up without perspective

    I turn to the reliability of gravity
    We are all
    touched
    by this nakedness

    I turn to the majesty of the stars at night
    the spiraling Milky Way

Your mystery shines
the whole length of my body

I turn to the nature of the fruit tree
Your persistence astounds
all the chambers
of my heart

I turn to the symmetry of the cabbage spiraling open
In this lostness
I find a
firmness in you

The love of this planet is the knowing of delight and death

CONSTELLATIONS

Lay your head on my belly,
my breast
The rise and fall of breath comforts you
The garden of
my embrace full as a
plum tree in autumn

My fingers move through your hair
how beautiful you are
Life loves
all the wild
variations

Your tears flow
Your losses march out
onto the fields and forests
like fog
Your skin the apprehension
we all feel

Let your heart remember
its original openness
Let yourself get lighter in my arms
Loosen yourself like
Fall leaves
There is no escaping this
undressing

Let the ancient astronomers whisper
their good advice
Existence cuts across us brilliantly
The shooting star crazy with
seeking

You are not dusty, old, and reviled
You are a universe filled with
constellations
intelligent patterns
a sweet cluster of possibility

ORIGINAL INSTRUCTIONS

Our lives hinge on one another
original instructions written only everywhere!
The whole breadth of our bodies
lay together a super
nova of intelligent design

Motion oozed across leaves
cytoplasm of slime mold
foraging, remembering, growing
To human eyes, a simple splash
of coral-like shape and apricot color a
rest stop for curious minds and sometimes
trash and Frisbees left by children and dogs
Until her wisdom was discerned

Dispersed imagination sprouts torso and legs
the body of an ant! Dropping from logs and leaves
walking up trees
Mounds of forest detritus gathered
Vast materials moved
without spending any time
in traffic

Crossing into the next day's life
Peacock tails
waving like flags, over here!
Dazzling designs
Magnificent colors

without the use of dyes or pigments

Giant dangling earrings royal yellow ornaments
Pomelo strike the ground from great heights
with no damage
Push the brilliance of their skin through
even the most skeptical stare
hierarchically organized peel structure
new materials created for safety applications

Solitary Strigiformes, nocturnal black-eyed Owl
Serrated feather shapes like a comb, create no
noise or turbulence
Eloquent shapes inspire new fan and turbine
designs nearly
silent

In the churning water world
swarming fish
swimming in vortices
saving energy
Optimal positions for tight arrays of vertical-axis
wind turbines

Great Spirit of the Original Instructions that live
in the deep caves where blood pumps
Your time-tested patterns and strategies guide our
products, processes, and policies—new ways of living
well adapted to life on earth
a sophisticated vocabulary

Consummate Engineer, your handiwork far and wide
The secrets to survival
written in all places

I leave the road
the luminous sky leaves with me
my heart filled with anticipation

CARESS

In this seaside village
I draw spaciousness
from the fog
when along the bay trail
a bird call shrills
harsh as a rusted piccolo

In this seaside village
I move through a day of my own hazards
Tempestuous drivers and near-miss collisions
End-of-life losses blooming
Abusive words falling with a meaningless thud
Fog horns and car horns
blatant cymbal crash

In this seaside village
I strain to be charmed by Orpheus' song
Carry wonder's particular
optimistic weight
Deep and unashamed supplication
May all beings be well

What story will be made in the
unmapped time ahead?
I live the shallow breath of
being fleeting
Not the web or the broken strand but
the impulse for connection

Trailing my hand in the
rippling sea
I float as if the bobbing
seal might
caress me
I want her to

ACKNOWLEDGMENTS

I began with a sense of curiosity fueled by data and concepts provided by the Intergovernment Panel on Climate Change (IPCC) and illustrations by Michael Mann and Lee Kump in *Dire Predictions: Understanding Climate Change,* as well as Jeff Nesbit's book entitled, *This is the Way the World Ends.* I was profoundly inspired by the work of Janine Benyus, science writer and founder of the Biomimicry Institute, whose positivity and practical direction to look to the living world as "mentor, model, and measure" provided a deep and abiding antidote to the troubling dynamics of our planet in its current season of winter.

I was moved by the caregivers who allowed me the deep privilege of participating in the care of their loved ones at end-of-life and to those loved ones who granted me the opportunity to accompany them during a vulnerable time of transition and need. I thank you.

To the poets of my heart who succor every grief; Yehuda Amichai, Louise Glück, Alice Walker, Robert Bly, Jack Gilbert, Elizabeth Bradford, Ilya Kaminsky, Julia Cameron, Constance Rowell Mastores, Maurya Simon, Adrienne Rich, and so many more, I bow to the greatness of your views of the world.

Great thanks to my friends, Marian Jensen and Alanna Zrimsek, whose generous, affirming, and astute guidance was invaluable.

www.ingramcontent.com/pod-product-compliance
Lightning Source LLC
Chambersburg PA
CBHW022106040426
42451CB00007B/146